Let The Sun Shine In

spoken word and poetry

Rhea "RheaSunshine" Carmon

Iris Press Chapbook Series
Oak Ridge, Tennessee

ISBN: 978-1-60454-512-8

Cover Art: Emma Goldsmith

Copy Editing: Tama Brisbane,
Poet Laureate of Stockton, CA

Book Design: Robert B. Cumming, Jr.

Iris Publishing Group, Inc
www.irisbooks.com

Contents

Preface

In the fall of 1999, I was invited to Café Noir at Knoxville College. I was super nervous. Having never read any of my poetry aloud, I worried about how I would be received. I shared a song and a poem that night and to say I was in love is an understatement. I loved the feeling of being nervous in front of an audience, the way the microphone allowed me to take over the room, but mostly I loved that I could express my deepest feelings without judgement. I found my therapist and she was the microphone.

Since that day, I have written constantly. Each time I allow myself the time to be vulnerable with a page, I am catapulted into a new understanding of life, love, self, and expression. I write for therapy, and honestly poetry has not only saved my life, but other people's lives as well. I want to share a few poems that have truly been a lifeline to me during this journey.

When I first started writing, I never thought I would hold the office of Poet Laureate of the City of Knoxville, nor did I believe that anybody would want to publish my work. Nonetheless, I continued writing and pushing myself to be better. I can only hope you can see the growth in my writing over the years and that these words provide as much strength, courage, and sunshine to you as they have for me.

I am forever thankful to my parents, Ernestine Abernathy and the late Theodore J. Scruggs for allowing me the capacity to be creative. I have grown so much as an artist over the years and I owe so much to my remarkable husband for never trying to extinguish my flame. I also want to thank my friends, family, and supporters for always being there to champion me forward. This book is dedicated to Adaiah and Isaiah, my sons. May they always find comfort in my words and know that I push them to be their creative self wherever it may take them.

Come In!

You have no idea who you are looking at, most days
    looking through
Wish you could see the world the way that I do
But you're too busy looking for all the things wrong
    to see all the things right
While I am open eyes seeing sunshine peeking
    through rain clouds
I am open heart loving even when love isn't
    returned with the same consideration
I am open ears listening to your feelings
I am open legs for the one God provided and open
    womb for the sons of sunshine
That bring brightened smiles and renewed belief in
    miracles
I am open spirit for the words of the Most High to
    flow through this
Open mouth, speaking life to all who will receive and
    for those that won't I will sing
An open lament for the death of your closed mind
Look closely and you will see that life has not always
    been good to me
I have learned to be open for change and business
    at all times
Each day is a blessing whether it is opened by a kiss
    or a cry
I refuse to close myself off to the beauty
    that surrounds me
I am open to criticism and open to praise
I am open to grace, amazing grace shall always be my
    song of praise
I am open to salvation needed daily to make it
And open to the poetry that God gave to provide
    my freedom from the shackles of unrealized dreams
Open your ears so you can hear me,
    my heart is screaming for you to know that
I am open arms ready to provide a real hug
That melts away your troubles and soothes your bad
    day

I am an open book, read me and you will see me
As open to possibilities and positivity
And most of all the reality of the world I live in
A world not ready for me or my open mind
Causing me to be open to pain and selfishness
Making me open to the ugly truth that
Open containers get used until they are empty
So I allow this poetry to refill me constantly
So I can keep myself open to the kind of love that
    loves me openly
Holding nothing back
I open the door to be seen completely as me
Come in!

What's in a Name?

One of the fondest moments I can remember
Is the day I looked up Rhea in the Encyclopedia
The book was wider than I
Yet as an addict of knowledge I attached myself to this
book
Only to find disappointment in the pages
As I searched I learned that Rhea
Was a flightless bird
And pronounced Ree-ah.
My devastation grew as I began to identify
Myself according to my name.

So I took my newfound knowledge
To the source of my nomenclature
And with boldness proclaimed his inability
To accurately pronounce my name
And still with tears in my eyes,
I said
"I'm all wrong and I can't fly"
And instead of responding with anger
He comforted my pride with a hug
Assured me, that he knew what he was doing
When he named me Ray-ah
Because not only could I fly
But I
Was a mother to the gods
And with his words my identity changed
From the ugly, gray and awkward flightless bird
To that of a radiant godly mother
And I learned that day that he was gentle
Caring sincerely for his child
Not offended that the encyclopedia
Disagreed with his level of knowledge
On that day, he gave me my wings
And I began to soar.

Eternal Life

I want to live forever
I want to dwell in moments of sincere bliss
Until the day I close my eyes
And go to meet my maker
Then I want to live forever
In the memory of those moments
Shared as family stories
Because I changed somebody's life
Made it a little better than it was before
I came along
I want to be a legend
To the women in my family
Young and old
And even those unborn
I want to be an example
For all believers of faith through storms, test and trials
I want to create in every thought
Through the words on these pages
Take my mother and father
Into forever with me
Share infinity with the woman so close
That sometimes she is me
The epitome of what friend should be
She cradles me in her mind
Delicately loving the woman I was
And am to be
I want to carry young poets on my shoulders
Into a destiny
I cannot live to see
But I will live forever
In the words that describe me
Pure and real
A lover of logos and rematos
A worshipper
Let my praise for the Most High live on forever
With me
For as long as Thank You Jesus
Can be uttered I will live on

In His praises
I want to live forever in poetry
For poetry is me
And can never be stopped
Terminated or erased it is the best witness of the soul
Working frantically to express life
And as long as life needs expression
Poetry and I will breathe
And live forever.

Beauty

A system of lies
Has been built to despise you,
So you don't realize
The gift of freedom possessed in your eyes
Surprise
You have been hypnotized
By the bouncing booty on your television screen
It seems mean
But what does it really mean
When a baby's mother is only fourteen
Thirteen and twelve
Our young men are steady filling up the jails
And those that can help
Stand by and say
"Oh well, as long as I have mine
Then to hell with tomorrow's generation"
But who will we trust to run this nation
Since you been blinded by the idea
That you're a man
Because of the of the size of your rims
Or the length of your diamond chain
Lack of vision making you insane
Stand up and be a real man
Bring something back to the community
Something of value or worth to be used
For our betterment rather than our endangerment
You have an opportunity to change this world
See treasure and create peace
Because demons only see green
Don't allow them to live in you
Change the vision
God gave you to create beauty
Exploiting the woman's humanity
Making a mother a whore and rapping about it
Snatching the ability she holds to nurture
Just to sell records
Women no longer have to sell their bodies on the
    street

They can do it on BET
And it's okay
Mother's can't teach their daughters of self worth
Because their fathers
Rap about windows and walls
Making females crawl
And lower their self-esteem
Till they forget what it is to dream
Cycle it through the world
So that innocence is lost for even little girls
Through Lucifer's beats and manipulation
You kill the reason for musical manifestation
Wake up to a world that is crying for attention
We need spirituality not so much pollution
Your money making is a spiritual dilution
Concocted by those seeking our execution
Presidents send people to die for no cause
Except those seen by his own demons
I have a problem accepting that there is a valid reason
And you remain silent
Open your eyes
A free mind is the best situation
For an integration
Of the souls imagination
With the LORD's intervention
Let's return to the true meaning of creation
Knowing God pulled us out of His Son
Now we are destined
To create His position
In the midst of a world needing revelation
And all that Burberry and Gucci
Don't help the cause called revolution
Repetition is how people learn so listen
You have an opportunity to change this world
Our people die daily
Of major and minor diseases in areas that music
Reaches before medication does.
Limbs lost for the cost of the gems on your fingers
And chains, stop being a slave, and rearrange your
    mind
To bring about change.

Trust that we are beings of sound
And if you are going to live up to who you are
Let every sound you make uplift,
        make someone else a better person
Stop running your mouth to hear yourself talk
Spit words of ramah that inspire
Rather than just words of logos that can be heard
But not change a life
Beauty is in the eye of the beholder
So close your eyes
Listen to the world's cries
Free your mind
And see the ending God sees
An entire world set free
Beauty.

Listen Closely

It's been 23 years since my father took his journey
    into eternity
I learned many life lessons from his existence
And gained crucial knowledge from him
    dying
We will all leave here
Death is part of life
When our loved ones
    are no longer with us,
    will we remember their voices?
I can remember his eyes and his smile
Recall frequently everything he ever taught me
However over the years, I have had to turn off the radio
Put in a lot of effort and prayer to hear his voice
A soft velvet tenor escaping his vocal chords
On the mornings we drove to school
Yet sometimes this world is too loud for me to hear
His whisper and I fear sometimes that if I don't find
    silence
I will never have the chance to search my memories
    again
I remember how his gentle voice soothed me
As tears streamed down my face
From pain, internal and external
And as I struggle sometimes in life I still need to hear his
    voice
Like rain outside my window, it has the ability to calm
    my soul
I sat at his feet
Learned to listen and internalize
How he would fatherly philosophize
I didn't know to memorize his voice
Didn't realize how important it is to remember
How those God blesses us to love, touch our lives
    with their voice
I struggle, I can't always remember how he
    sounded,
When he said "I love you"

Though I remember he did say it often
And I can sing the notes he harmonized with
Each time we worshipped together in the car on
    school days
But can't remember how he sounded singing them
I loved him with all I knew love to be
Yet the simplest thing like the vibration
Of his voice through air to my ears, evades my
    memory
And he could sing so beautifully
In this world of technology
We allow email and text messaging to replace sound
If one of the most important things to do when a
child is in the womb
Is to allow them to hear your voice, why do we feel
    we should mute
The impact of the voices of those we love
Those voices are our reason to know it is okay to go
    out in the world
They keep us reminded that we always have someone
    in our corner
So now I call my mother daily, allow her to hear my
    voice
Talk to her grandsons, so they can hear how she
    sounds
When she tells them they are handsome and will
    always be loved
I sing to my sons and dance in the living room
Because we are not just living life we are making
    memories
I talk to my friends on the phone or go and visit
Send video messages to long distance family
I have learned to connect
Listen closely as they speak and write the memories
    for me to recall
I remember music from my entire lifetime
But at my age, I still struggle to hear my father
I am different now
Understanding that I cannot change the past
I can create a better future with the soundtrack of
    their voices

Etched perfectly into my psyche
I show I care by listening now, taking in the beauty of
    sound and silence
I create moments where my sons will have smiles as
    they think of me
So I can continue driving, turn off my radio, and
    always hear the voices
Of those I love the most.

A Prayer of Desperation

Lord, I want to write a poem
I want to write a poem
That speaks, that sings, that teaches
The world the importance of keeping you
At the forefront of our success
I want to write a poem
That tells the world that I am not perfect
And never will be
But because you love me
You allow me the capacity to write a poem
That touches my mother and lets her
Know that I admire the woman she
Was, is, and is yet to be
I want to write a poem that testifies
Of all the places I can walk after the
Doctors told me I would die once
And the doctors told me I would die twice
And the doctors told me I might not see
So I want to write a poem that yells at the doctors
"Look at me now"
I want to write a poem that makes poets pick up their
    pens
And write a poem from their hearts
And shows them that the power is not in their scores
But in their gift and they need to use it
To change the world
God, I want to write a poem
That brings forth miracles
Heals hearts and minds
And brings joy in times of trouble
God I want to write a poem

I want to write a poem that makes you
Stand up from your throne and snap your fingers
As you sing Amazing Grace
I need to write a poem that reaches beyond
The grave and makes my father proud of the woman
I have become

I want to write a poem that is honest
Sometimes I want to quit and have thought about
    giving up
But I want to write a poem that gives me the strength
    to go on
Energizes my sometimes weary spirit
And reminds me why I pick up the pen
And want to write a poem
That knows what love is and tells him that
I love him
I want to write a poem that delivers
Addicts from their addiction
And makes young people pay attention
I want to write a poem that whispers
Much like your voice
In the midst of the storms, bringing peace
To the unrest of our souls
And makes us whole
Lord, I want to write a poem
That causes an earthquake of creativity and
An explosion of laughter
I want to write a poem that lives
The life that's not easy but finds a way to
Survive and supplies
My sons with enough power to change the world
After I close my eyes
I want to write a poem that makes You
Open a mic in heaven when I get there because
I want to write a poem of praise
One that uses all your names and bows down to
    worship
El Shaddai, Jehovah Jireh, Elohim, Yeshua and
    Yaweh
God I want to write a poem that breaks traditional
    barriers and
Makes it okay to KRUMP dance in church
Because sometimes it really does take all that to
Keep the devil from weighing you down
See I want to write a poem that makes Martin
Wish he had written a poem instead of dreaming a
    dream

And still I want to write a poem
That makes dreams come true
One that displays you
Forces people to move when they need to
And spark an undying passion for you
Lord, I want to write a poem that bleeds the blood of
    Jesus,
Jews, slaves, witches, New Yorkers, Haitians,
Japanese women and children,
New Orleans, Hiroshima, Nagasaki,
Iraq, Kuwait, Pearl Harbor, Afghanistan,
South Central LA, the Watts, Mississippi, Knoxville,
Black bodies fallen in the street,
And I just want to write a poem that speaks,
That sings,
That teaches
So, speak through me
Let me be your pen.

Free Dumb

If I could package the feeling I get when I'm in His
     glory
I would—sell it on the street corner like crack
Then everybody would be a glory addict
Saying things like, "Man, I will pray for you"
For just one more hit
Can you imagine it
Jesus freaks standing on the corner
Selling worship experiences
That take you out of this world
And keep you coming back for more
And more and more glory
People will stop wanting to work
Hate, war and divide
Because everybody would be high
On Jesus that is.
But I couldn't call it glory
Because people are afraid to truly let God
Have control of their lives
So I would have to call it something cool
And enticing like Escape, because
It will take you away to a place
Of peace and sweet release
And set you completely free
Or possibly, I could call it just that FREE
Since salvation is FREE
And you might have to work for glory
But it doesn't cost any money
So it is FREE
I see it now
FREE HEADS coming up to me, the FREE dealer
Of the streets
And asking, how much for just one more dose of
FREE
I've tried to stop, but the Holy Ghost got me
And like a good dealer I would say
Lift you hands and repeat
"Lord I love you", "You are all I need"

"Bathe me in your FREE"
"So I can be who you want me to be"
Oh can't you see it
People lined up on the street
Chanting praises for another dose of FREE
And then I would break it to them that this
Feeling could last eternally, if they would only
Choose God to be their FREE LORD
And I would bring them on
So that soon there would be FREE dealers
In every city
Because this is how I think
Contrary to what the world sees now
I guess that is what makes me a dreamer
But remember, so was Joseph
MLK and C.S. Lewis
So I'm in good company
And it might help the world if you would all become
Dreamers with me
Have a vision, write it down,
Be crazy enough to believe
And maybe we could all dream the world FREE.

The Love of My Life

I Love you more than even I know
You take me to places beyond my imagination
Allowing me to secrete knowledge of misunderstood
    things
Opening my mind to see all that evades me
Drawing me into you and helping me realize
That with you expression is all I need to survive
Letting me know that as God expresses love
My heart beats and I breathe
Breaths of air that nourish each cell
Of my body to be engulfed by you.
Giving birth to love for more than hip hop
I find peace in expression
Through our children of music, poetry and
Rhythms that speak to me
Of my ancestry and my love for the drum beat
Knowing through that beat emerges
Strength transferred over oceans and time
To the day I first realized that you
Alone would be the love of my life.
You got me doing back flips over sunrises
Somersaults over full moons
Walking on the leaves of trees
My heart skipping over rivers of me
For in loving you I find peace
Ever flowing through my mind to the first time
I heard you echo through the walls of my mother's
    womb
I was born to love you
As my father sang consolation to my spirit
In the form of Sam Cook's coming change
Cause I was born by the river
Loving you, and who knew that love
Would grow to include a sister weeping over death
And cataclysmic psychedelic rain falling
In a story of spoken creations occurring before time
I realize that tribute is due
To those that have enhanced this love affair with you

Dickenson, Hughes, Grand Master Flash, Paul the
    Apostle, Timbaland,
Hathaway, Sheila E., Iceberg Slim, Nina Simone, the
    Neptunes, Common,
David the Psalmist, and John, Big Boi, Kenny, India Arie,
Roberta Flack, Mary J, the Roots, Alex Haley,
Coltrane, D'Angelo, Franklin, Mozart,
Lauryn Hill, Frost, Prince, M.J., Poe, Heatwave
Doug E. Fresh, Hammond, Jessica Care-Moore,
Walker, Whodini, Keats, Kweli, Patti LaBelle, Big Daddy
Kane, and Beau Sia T.J., Stevie Wonder, Omari, Aretha,
Andre, Dunbar, Gaye, Swizz Beatz, Ice T, D.J. Quik,
Faith, Robika, Handel, Black Greeks, Saul Williams,
my husband, my sons, and Jesus.
For you were in the beginning and without you there
    is no me
You alone encompass all that I love
And that is why loving you makes everything alright
Everything is Everything
As long as the world realizes
That in my eyes everything is you.
You open those eyes to clues
Of who I am
King of Kings makes me a Queen
Lord of Lords makes me a duchess
So I rule the world through my love for you.
You give me power
Nothing can describe you
Or begin to encompass all that you are to me and
The world's very existence
For in the beginning was the word
And the word was with God
And the word was God
You are the word
For there is nothing made without you
So in loving you I find existence
Depth, love, and breadth
You are my peace, my voice, my blackness
Whether it exist through scripture, song, a beat or
    simply poetry
You are the love of my life.

My Soul Cries Out

The sound of a soul crying out
The sound of a soul crying out
Me say Oh,
My soul cries out

My soul cries out because a white judge
Just put a black boy in prison for the rest of his life
Imprisoning not only his body
But also his mind
My soul cries out cause the system won this time

The sound of a soul crying out
The sound of a soul crying out
Me say Oh,
My soul cries out

My soul cries out because I have sisters that actually
    believe
They're prettier with a weave
Not know that they're the most beautiful woman
God created
Whether their hair is relaxed or dreaded
And my soul cries out because my brothers are too
    worried
About the bling, bling, and getting some booty
To actually be my king and respect me.

Can you hear the sound of my soul crying out?
Can you hear the sound of my soul crying out?

My soul cries out because when you see me
You really don't see me
All you see is my dark skin and nappy hair
And you dare not see my heart of gold
But the racist mentality is getting old.
And my soul cries out because
A mother isn't a mother anymore
And her children sit, baby sat by the T.V.

When will they see, that their brains are slowly
Drifting away and with their minds
Our future.
My soul cries out because ignorant people refuse
    education
And learned people refuse to be educated
They need spiritual knowledge
The kind that can't be learned in the walls of a college
Or else our nation dies
Denying the cries of our spirits.

The sound of a soul crying out
The sound of my soul crying out
Me say Oh, my soul cries out
For change, change, change
Aren't you tired of the same thing?
A world that needs change and no one will step
    forward
I refuse to be silent anymore
This is the sound of my soul crying out
Me say OH

My soul cries out for freedom in the minds of men
My soul cries out for love in the hearts of men
My soul cries out for hope, in the eyes of men
My soul, your soul, our souls cry out.

The sound of a soul crying out
The sound of our souls crying out
We say Oh,
And our souls cry out!

Lyrical Abacus

My mind works in beats
Of poetry and numbers
All I consider and love can be
Added to knowledge
Subtracted by boundaries
Multiplied by love
And divided by time
Proofs made of conversations and vulnerability
Tested by relationship
Each measure plays a part
In my lyrical equation
Rhythm provides the life source
Necessary to express beauty
Equaling me plus one
Higher than infinity
What I can't explain with numbers
I find in words
And when words evade me
I fall into the aftermath…

Square Up MS

I didn't know you were here
With me all along
Causing more problems than solutions
You were hiding somewhere in the crevices of my
    mind
Making me less of the woman that I wanted to be
You abused my energy
For your own sick, twisted plan
You make me weak whenever you want to
Decide when I will sleep and when I need to go
    without it
You torture me incessantly
Invisible to all but your results are evident
"I'm making it"—now becomes my mantra
Because I'm doing everything I can daily to fight you
Trying to win a battle with myself
Because you reside somewhere up there
In the part of me that I can't see without the
    technology
MRIs and dye are the only things that reveal you to
    the world
You are rattling around in my brain
At times making me question my sanity
Because when you are in control
I feel outside of myself
Watching myself struggle to do things that normally
    come easy
Thinking
Questioning
Why me? What did I do to deserve this type of
    relationship
This type of thorn in my flesh
This punishment for
Who knows what I could have done to deserve your
    presence
I can't get rid of you
Monkey on my back
Trying hard to keep my thoughts and faith on track

I know I'm healed but
Yesterday it didn't really manifest itself the way I
	needed it to
Instead you showed up
Trying to make me doubt the God I serve and
	become desperate enough
To give up but that is not in my personality
And you might change a lot of things but you cannot
	change that part of me
I'm writing you out
Letting you know that although we are joined
	together through nerves and chromosomes
I will never be your slave
I will do me without failing because all I do is Win
So square up MS, you got a fight on your hands.

Through the Clouds

Sometimes I wonder where I went
Lost in the roles that I play the jobs that I hold
I don't always know which way to turn to land on my
feet
But I refuse to stop pushing
Something about this life is hard to understand if you
have never lived it
I have stitched my life to another and now I have to
wonder
If our hearts will beat in sync to accomplish all my
dreams and his
Where am I in all of this?
I've lost sight of who I am and just taken on the role
of wife
Maybe mother
Maybe poet
Maybe teacher
I'm not sure I am wearing all these hats well and I am
struggling to still look fly
Even when I haven't had a chance to look into the
mirror
Just to remind myself who I am and what I look like
And this is not the first or last time this will happen
I am constantly becoming more aware of where I am
in this life
Lost at first but then I return to the place in my heart
that I tucked myself
Offer her the hand to emerge again and find the new
me
Different but somehow more beautiful than when I
put her away to be what they needed
I lose myself and find myself constantly
The journey of a woman dedicated to be all God
called me to be
I'm not the person I was yesterday and tomorrow I
will not be the person I am today
I make mistakes, not often but it happens
I am not always what they need but I am always trying

Struggle has become my best friend and I attempt to
    figure out who I will be today
Daughter
Maybe Friend
Maybe Survivor
Maybe Dreamer
Wondering if you will ever be able to understand my
    pain
Questioning pain that never seems to go away
I am still changing, still finding a way to grow and
    believe
When I'm barely getting by, trying to be more than
    the tears streaming down my face
I am learning to always grow and find myself each
    time I lose myself
I was afraid I would never find me again
But here I am,
More me than I ever thought I could be
RheaSunshine peaking through the clouds
I can finally see me again, can you!?

Beauty is Sacrifice

She walks on feet backwards with determination
Calloused with confidence she strolls and we have
    been known to look at those feet and
    call them ugly
Never understanding the beauty
    in each step that she takes
Have you ever seen her on pointe?

For it is at this point that beauty makes itself known
And the abuse done to her feet
    becomes worth the pain that she felt each time
She stretched herself past what God created
    and made herself the dancer that we can all
    appreciate

I never really liked feet until I looked at hers
She was ashamed of the years of pain but
I saw beauty and started to see more in feet than
    anyone could have ever realized
My foot phobia had begun at an early age
    as I looked at my mothers
I vowed to never allow my feet to become so
    calloused and ashy,
Never wanted my feet to
    see the torture hers had gone through,
So I made monthly visits to the spa
    and gave myself regular pedicures
Not knowing that those feet had walked miles
I wasn't capable of understanding
She cared so much for us that she never had time to
    make trips to the spa
Never gave the money to the young Asian woman
    behind the counter to make sure her
    feet were beautiful
Because she was so dedicated to
    making sure that our lives were beautiful
So she walked in shoes sometimes too small

Stood on those feet as they ached and cooked dinner for
    those ungrateful...
Too ungrateful to at times get down and lotion her
    feet
The child that would go to bed with her mother but
    wear socks that came up to my knees
Because I didn't want to feel the touch of her feet
And now I see, that those feet are beautiful
Because what would you sacrifice for those that you
    love
Its almost like Christ, punished His perfection for our
    salvation
He allowed himself to be battered so that we could
    emerge beautiful
And now I understand that is what they have done to
    their feet
Sacrifice is beautiful tied in a ballet slipper,
She stretched her arches to the point that her
    feet now appear backwards
But when she dances, we all awe at the beauty that has
    emerged from her pain
Sacrifice is beautiful beat into the souls of a mother's
    shoes
She pushes herself beyond
    limits to walk roads not yet travelled and create
    opportunity for her children
And when she smiles at their accomplishments,
    we revel in the beauty that has emerged from her
    pain

Sacrifice is beautiful nailed to a cross,
Savior born free of sin, yet taking all on
      His shoulders,
      His feet bore the affliction of all as He pressed upon
      the nail just to achieve breath
And when we praise,
      we give glory for the beauty that
      we have become because of where
He allowed His feet to take Him

Eyes now opened I am no longer afraid of or turned
    off by feet
I am reminded each time she dances, or walks in
    sandals without lotion,
    or He blesses me
That feet tell a story of what you are willing to give
    for love and that is
Beautiful.

For Art's Sake

(dedicated to Art Smith R.I.P.)

I never really thought my story was valid
Always thought the power came in my delivery
Nobody wants to read my words
They only want to hear my voice
But art is more than delivery
Art is the press it takes to get to the page
The moments when nobody is around
    and inspiration is your only friend
Art is the story behind the poem and the picture
It's the space between the words
My power comes in my art, in my head, in my heart
Where it all adds up and becomes a beautiful
    solution to the complicated equation of my life
Art is finding love right in front of me, when I was
looking down
It's the hands of a child meant for greatness reaching
    out for mine
Art is the moment when they see the lesions on my
    MRI
It's when I accept that they will never go away
The needle in my arms, my hips, my thighs and my
    stomach
The shock my body took from those needles
The daily pills that make me feel outside myself
The child growing in spite of the medicine
It's more lesions in spite of the medicine
Art is the fear that they will never find a way to stop
    the pain
It's the inspiration to share the stage with other
    women sharing stories of their own art
Contemplating coming home from a job I love
Because the stress is causing more lesions
It's finding a medicine that may work, then being
    denied
Taking the chance to be pumped with steroids
And an infusion medicine that may cause a brain
    disease that could take me away from my blessings

Its hearing its time
I learned art in a small classroom
Writing poems, asking to be accepted as a poet
Begging to be seen as art
Art taught me, that I am art
My story is valid and the only thing that makes my art
    real.

The Greatness Within

I was never meant to apologize
    for the greatness that is within me
I was never meant to shrink or be small
    in the presence of men
I was only meant to radiate like sunshine
Every word a solar flare flickering to ignite a flame
Today I found myself saying sorry for the space that I
    occupy
Apologizing for being me
And it made me feel broken
Like something in me is wrong
But I want to be healed
Refusing to apologize for existing as the one God
    created
I will not apologize that my warmth, my size, my
    smile, or my words which may
    at times make you feel small
I will only ask you to find the greatness within
    yourself
And never apologize for being you

The Invitation

I invited him to make love to me
Sent him a private invitation to the party that is my life
Truth, I could have had a party without him, but I'm
    so glad
He showed up with a ring in hand and took mine in
    his
He is my person, sees me for the woman I am
Made vows to love me through thick and thin
And I have watched him live those vows 1000
    times and we still have so many more years to go
He completes me, the gift God had wrapped for me
I'm no less of a powerful woman,
I have come to realize that everything before him
    was leading to these times
When sharing my stage wouldn't seem so hard
And changing who I am allows me to let down my
    guard
Now I dance like only he is watching because he is
    the only one that matters
I have no problem dropping it likes it's hot
Giving all I got and being weak is not as bad as it
    seems
When he's holding me
He brings out the best in me
Let's me know that in this party we can and will be
    weird together
Teach our boys that being weird is perfectly okay
So on the day when this party music skips
Neither one of us splits
Cause our party won't stop
He put his love on top and got me doing things
Like dressing up
Just to put a smile on his face
Help me determine when to change my ways
He's too much for me sometimes, but just enough all
    the time
Never perfect but perfect for me
Helped me see me completely, loving me totally

He's made just for me,
So sometimes we disagree and wonder if this was
    really meant to be
But I see it in his eyes, each time he kisses me
So we gon' ride this ride until the wheels fall off
Not caring who wants to join our party
Because I invited him to make love with me
And we did!

Conversations

Let me learn your walk, your talk
Your way of thinking
Though different from mine
Let me consider changing
Let me decide that I love you
Let me not change
And you still know that I care for you
Let us balance each other into the people that we
     want be
As we share words and conversations
Of greatness trapped and circulating between us
Let us create poetry in these moments of forever growth
Water my soul with your openness
Fertilize my mind with the richness of life
Let me be the sunshine
To harvest beauty in the diversity
Open your voice that I may hear your words
Let them slide into the canals of my ear
Provide some clarity of how I should think of you
Let your words and passion
Teach a new way to journey to love
Let love for humanity win
Let my heart be shown in my silence
Or my voice
Let you see me, for the person that I am
Let me see you, for who you are
Let us walk together
Let us join together
Let us change a world that wants to keep us separate
As we find the way to communicate
Let us see life in the eyes of one another
And choose to keep looking for it
Let us look for love rather than understanding
Let us be broken together, human
Let us experience utopia when we share
Come and talk with me
Teach me your walk, teach me your talk
Teach me you
And I will teach you, me!

Morning Meditation

Looking on a pond
I watch a small red finch sing
Beautiful freedom

In the midst of rain
He calls out a praise to God
Nothing stops his song

That teaches me peace
Nothing to worry about
God always provides

Can I be that bird
Trusting that God is with me
Taking care of me

Whatever I need
He promised to supply it
I need only trust

Fly free little finch
Not a worry in the world
You taught me today

Letting go is peace
Freedom is a state of mind
I will trust the LORD.

He has never failed
Keeping every promise
Offering me grace

Outside my window
He lets me see His glory
Looking on a pond

Birth Right

A poem for all that fight for the right to breathe

I was born with fire in my veins
Headstrong and destined for greatness
Power behind black eyes
Breath in lungs
Fresh and purposeful
I cried for my mother and it was beautiful
Announced to the world my beginning
My birth right to exist and breathe
My birthright to grow, stand, walk, run, sleep
Without losing the right to pull oxygen from air
To satisfy life
You have taken what cannot be returned
As I struggled to receive my birthright
I cried for my mother and it was revolution
It became the voice of a nation of black people
Seeking to reclaim the right to breathe
Our first right to life, a cry that screams hope for
    America
When you stopped my breath you did not stop our
    voice
You only ignited the fire
And it will not be extinguished.

Medicine

A merry heart is good like a medicine
So as much as I love to laugh
I should be able to fight off the autoimmune disease
Headaches, muscle cramps, and joint pain
Heartache and feeling inadequate
I can do none of those things
But I have learned to enjoy my laugh
I have learned that it makes my tolerance for the pain
    more bearable
So when given the opportunity, I laugh
Out loud, allow my voice to fill the room
Maybe create an infectious ripple that makes others
    join the chorus
Because I feel it so deep in my soul
It is my way to release the stress and heal my mind
This laugh takes control and becomes everything to
    my world in the moment
I'm not exactly sure when I realized that my laugh is
    boisterous
Or when I questioned how it makes others feel
That I am so free to laugh so loud and never hold
    back
Bubbling sounds from my soul to teach
The freedom of self-acceptance
The acknowledgement of my difference and reality of
    its beauty
Sometimes, I just laugh to keep from crying
Other times, I laugh until I cry because the tears need
    to be released
And what better way for them to burst forth than
    from a smile
That became active like a volcano
And erupted from my gut to give way for cleansing
    grace
No matter what, my laugh will never be as astonishing
    as
The sound of laughter catapulting from the lungs of
    my sons

When they laugh the entire world is made perfect
New creation each time, they find the freedom to let
    joy overflow
I have taught them something by laughing out loud
A speechless lesson, I hope they never forget
As life becomes full of reasons to snatch your smile
    and your confidence
I hope they remember their mother laughing
I hope they find comfort in throwing their head back,
    hand on their stomach
Hearing a bellow from their soul and healing
    themselves
With the medicine that I teach them to make
Each time I laugh.

After the Black

There are few things that are obvious from a first glance
    at me
The most obvious is that I am black
And I suppose you could stop there
You could allow that to put a wall between you and I
Or you could see it as an immediate connect with me
Whichever you choose, I fear that you will have only
    scratched the surface of my essence
What will you do after the black?
After you have judged whether I match or clash your
    perception
Following that initial reaction, will you care to know my
    story?
Because you can't know immediately that I identify as a
    heterosexual
You can't know that I am married with children
That I wish daily that my children could meet the man
    that raised me
And climb into his lap to call him Pops
That my mother speaks to me every time I cross her
    mind because her spirit is connected to me
And she is my first hero
There is no way for you to know, I see the world in
    poetry and numbers
Because they are real and tangible
I express my love in one of these two ways to every
    person in my life
What will you miss if you never make it past the black?
How many hugs that can change your day or mood will
    you miss out on?
How much inspiration and strength will you fail to ever
    see?
How many problems will you never solve?
How much understanding will you miss?
How much love?
If you only see me as a comrade or foe, have you truly
    looked?

I am broken by the people that spread hatred through
    their gaze
Judging, pulling triggers or closing doors
Forgetting to see human before difference
Spreading lies and division without first thinking golden
Finding reasons to remove a story by only looking
Skin Deep
Religion Deep
Party Deep
Sexuality Deep
Paycheck Deep
For whatever you have chosen you're black to be
What will it take for you to see after it
To see one another as humanity
To know that somebody has loved or been loved by
    another
Looked up at the same sky and seen the same sun
Gazed into the night and shared the same stars
Closed their eyes to sleep or die and met the same
    darkness
We are all looking for the light
Looking through mirrors to see ourselves as more
Than just a list of black that somebody may not accept

I've learned to love myself
My dark skin and coiled hair, I find power in its energy
I don't always fit in where it seems I should
I keep quiet on issues until I can write about them
I struggle to let people in to love me, but I give love freely
Trusting that I will never run out of love for myself
I fight my body against its attempts to break down daily
I am a survivor of more than this blackness
My father taught me that I was black and beautiful
Making sure that I understood there is more after the
    black
There is beauty deeper than this melanin
I will never allow myself to stop there
Or even see it as a weakness or flaw
It is me as much as my quirky personality
And belief in God without limitations
It is the understanding that I am made in that image

And I have no limitations
I am creation made perfect, just the way I am
So I embrace the flaws and imperfections
The hard days and the glorious transitions
There is nothing wrong with any part of who I am
Every attribute is marked with part of what exist
I am beautiful beyond the black
I am mother earth with treasures in my words
Giving birth to lightning, oceans, and fire
There is prophesy in my gardens
My father named me Rhea, calling me to motherhood
I am more than that initial glance
And you will never know until you see me
After the black.

It Is Well

—Performed with Knoxville Symphony Orchestra on July 4, 2021

Liberation, freedom, independence
All celebrated for providing the space to find self
To define who you are and who you will be
It is not a singular activity
We are constantly liberating and freeing ourselves
Our Ideas, pre-conceived notions, requirements
There is always growth
If you are not growing you're dying
Reexamining and reinventing yourself
Is the way to keep living
Flourishing as you become all that you should
Today we celebrate independence
Freedom to do what we want to do as a country
Red, white and blue
Taking responsibility for the consequences of our
    choices
It is well
It is changing the idea of equality without equity
Ceasing to look into the future without examining the
    past
It is living without restrictions and
The ability to express ourselves without fear of
    persecution
This freedom bought with the blood of our forefathers
Runs deeply through the blood of all that call
    themselves American
Though some would not feel the joy of it for years to
    come
We celebrate, this day as stepping stone for greatness
As a reason to believe we deserve liberation from
    tyrannical control
We play our drum as we hear it
Dance to the rhythm of our hearts beating, chanting
We hold these truths to be self-evident
That all men are created equal
What is all? What is men?

What is the creation?
What is equal?
When will we decide to let these truths
Ring true as the freedom we celebrate
Life, liberty and pursuit of those things that make us
    happy
What is happiness?
If we have not yet defined all and equal
Can we find it without seeing all as equal
Today we hold this truth high
Like fire in our hands
Light up the night sky with our love for country
Love for fellow American
Love for all, love for equality, love for life and liberty
Love for happiness, found when we truly let freedom
    ring.
It is well

Award-winning wordsmith Rhea "RheaSunshine" Carmon is a force that weaves passion, purpose, and power into poetry. For twenty years, RheaSunshine has traveled the nation, sharing her gift of the spoken word and facilitating self-expression, liberation, and healing. This art form has led her to touch lives at universities and educational institutions as well as civic engagements and festivals. She has opened for such artists as Nikki Giovanni, Macy Gray, and Saul Williams and the world constantly expands to make room for her gift.

Rhea "RheaSunshine" Carmon is the creator and Executive Director of the 5th Woman Cohort, which explores the stories of women. Regardless of race, women share the same experiences, fears, joys and more. The 5th Woman Cohort allows the participants to examine their various backgrounds without social and political barriers. Recently named the Poet Laureate of Knoxville, RheaSunshine strives to touch hearts and inspire people to share their own stories. She has published four chapbooks and has recorded three audio CDs. Her fourth book, *Through the Clouds*, explores her battle with Multiple Sclerosis. Not motherhood, MS, or any obstacle can slow this Renaissance woman down. As she has stated in her writing, she still has poems that she hasn't even written yet.

9 781604 545128